WHAT'S THE DEAL WITH..?

500 QUESTIONS TODAY'S STUDENTS ARE ASKING ABOUT THE BIGGEST ISSUES IN LIFE

BRIAN SCHULENBURG

 ZONDERVAN®

ZONDERVAN.com/
AUTHORTRACKER
follow your favorite authors

 youth
specialties

**youth
specialties**

What's the Deal With...?: 500 Questions Today's Students Are Asking About the Biggest Issues in Life
Copyright 2007 by Brian Schulenburg

Youth Specialties resources, 300 S. Pierce St., El Cajon, CA 92020 are published by Zondervan, 5300 Patterson Ave. SE, Grand Rapids, MI 49530.

Library of Congress Cataloging-in-Publication Data
Schulenburg, Brian.
  What's the deal with—? : 500 questions today's students are asking about the biggest issues in life / by Brian Schulenburg.
       p. cm.
  ISBN-10: 0-310-27364-1 (pbk.)
  ISBN-13: 978-0-310-27364-6 (pbk.)
  1. Life—Biblical teaching—Miscellanea. 2. Christianity—Miscellanea. I. Title.
  BS680.L5S38 2008
  230—dc22

                                                                    2007020504

All Scripture quotations, unless otherwise indicated, are taken from the *Holy Bible, Today's New International Version™*. TNIV®. Copyright 2001, 2005 by International Bible Society. Used by permission of Zondervan. All rights reserved.

Cover and interior design by SharpSeven Design

Printed in the United States of America

07 08 09 10 11 12 • 20 19 18 17 16 15 14 13 12 11 10 9 8 7 6 5 4 3 2 1

Jake and Becky Paul—thanks for being willing to take a risk and bring friends who desperately need Jesus to the Garage.

Charlie DeBeck—thanks for asking so many great questions that we had no choice but to begin a ministry that has become a movement.

Rick Krech, Terry Palmberg, Dave Peterson, and Rob Youngblood—thank you for joining me in the trenches on a weekly basis to answer students' questions.

Cindi Adams, our incredibly faithful server at Uno's week after week—over the past few years you've selflessly served thousands of students and made it possible for the adult leaders to relax and tend to the spiritual needs of our kids.

The students of Wooddale Church in Eden Prairie, Minnesota— these are *your* questions, and they're good ones. May you always find time to reach for the deepest things in life. You've made this youth pastor very proud of you.

Breanna, Chris, Jeremy, and Zach—you've sacrificed a lot to let Dad hang out with high school students. Thank you. The difference those hours have made in the lives of students is tremendous. My prayer is that these questions will be our questions too. I pray that, as a family, we'll continue to discover how wide and how deep and how great is the love of our God and how amazing he proves himself to be each and every day. I love you!

FOREWORD

Crisis in youth ministry, biblical illiteracy among Christian teenagers, the outflow of teenagers from the church after graduation—blah, blah, blah. You've heard the stats and stories. So there's no reason to scare you with more of them because you already know the deal, right?

The question isn't *if* there's a problem but *what* do we do about it? The age of youth ministry that focuses purely on event planning, light devotionals, and relational connection had its day, but now it's fallen flat on its face. (Fortunately, the fall was cushioned, thanks to a mouth full of marshmallows from a recent game of "chubby bunnies.")

If we're honest, we know deep down inside that the church can't compete with the world for our teenagers' attention. We don't have the bank account for it. No matter how big our youth ministry budgets are—they're nothing when compared to the budgets of MTV, iTunes, and MySpace. But on a deeper level, the

world can't compete with the church because the world doesn't have the truth.

Unfortunately, instead of teaching the truth outright, we try to out-entertain the professionals. We try to become event planners, game masters, and production directors who "call the show" and try to make every youth group meeting cued, tight, visceral, visual, and relational. Many youth ministries have become great at looking good, but teenagers are still leaving our churches. Why do you think there are fewer seniors in your youth group than freshmen? Because as hip as we try to be, we aren't as cool as we think we are.

Am I saying we should chuck the games, video clips, blaring music, and Xboxes and start lighting candles and chanting? No. In the words of Solomon, there is a time for everything. True wisdom is knowing what time it is.

It's time to add a new component to our youth ministry—real, raw conversation about God, life, the Bible, eternity, heaven, hell, abortion, homosexuality, sin, Jesus, and so on.

Not too long ago, I took a group of teenagers to the mountains of Colorado to film a reality series called *The GOSPEL Journey.* We had real teens—a Wiccan, an atheist, an agnostic, a Presbyterian, an Episcopalian, a minister's kid, and a city girl who didn't know what she believed—who had real questions. We tied in *Survivor*-type challenges with a journey through the story of the Bible and the gospel message. Part of the filming process allowed these teenagers and 20-somethings to ask any questions they wanted to about the gospel, God, sin, whatever. We soon discovered we didn't have enough film!

These young people stayed up until two or three in the morning almost every single night talking about the subjects of each day's gospel journey! They couldn't stop engaging, arguing, debating, and defending. While the conversations never got meanspirited, they were definitely intense!

During our time together, my only commitment to them was to answer them straight from the Bible as best I could. There were times I'd be praying while turning the pages of my Bible and asking God to help me remember where "that passage" was.

Soon after filming this video project, I found out about my buddy Brian's "Pizza and God Talk" event that he was running through his youth ministry at Wooddale Church. Brian told me how twice a month he'd have a night where students could bring their friends to a local pizza place and they'd talk about one relevant subject that tied in with God, theology, and life. Brian also told me how during these times he was more of a moderator than a preacher, and his only commitment was to answer the question of the night—straight from the Bible.

It clicked. This was a way for youth groups across America to have real, raw, and intense conversations about the issues that matter most. It's a way for the Scriptures to come to life for the average teenager. There's nothing like a debate or good old-fashioned disagreement to get the juices flowing! So I started promoting the "Pizza and God Talk" idea to thousands of youth leaders across America as a way to start adding a deeper element to their youth ministries.

Then Brian told me about this book, and something else clicked. *What's the Deal With...* is a way to bring that kind of robust discussion into any youth group meeting, Sunday school class, or small group. Even if you don't have a "Pizza and God Talk" night, any—perhaps even *every*—youth group meeting can have debate and discussion as key elements.

As you read this book, you may find yourself cutting a game or two in your youth program so you can bring up one of the following 500 questions to start a healthy discussion among your students. Your students might even stay late to continue the conversation! And someday maybe—just maybe—you'll find that you have just as many seniors in your youth group as you do freshmen.

But be warned: This book will force you to dive into *the* Book even more. Why? Because teenagers will ask questions you aren't prepared to answer. As they see you deal honestly with the Word of God and as they internally grapple with significant spiritual truth, you'll give them a reason to come back week after week and year after year. You'll cement their faith long term in a real, raw, and relevant way.

Buckle up.

—Greg Stier

Dare 2 Share Ministries

ACKNOWLEDGEMENTS

I can hardly believe I'm putting the finishing touches on my second book. Thanks be to God who birthed this book in a most unusual way. This book could not have been written without the movement of his Spirit in the lives of countless students. *What's the Deal With...* is really a special book. It's here because God moved in the lives of students who brought friends who needed Christ to our youth ministry. As a result, those friends saw their need for Christ and began asking great questions.

Thank you to the students of Wooddale Church. Thanks to Ryan Corrigan, Charlie DeBeck, Kyle Fox, Kevin Franske, Megan Hamilton, Steve Healy, Greg Krech, Rick Krech, Eric Lundin, Greg Overpeck, Terry Palmberg, Anthony Peterson, Aaron Rask, Breanna Schulenburg, Chris Schulenburg, Cyndi Schulenburg, Tom Segersin, Laura Stadler, and Matt Volenec for contributing at least one question to this book.

Thank you to the good folks at Youth Specialties/Zondervan who agreed to take another chance on this author. Jay Howver, Dave

9

Urbanski, and Roni Meek, once again you have stood behind a project and seen it through to the end. You are an author's delight. Thanks for believing in this project. May it be used to bless countless youth workers, families, and churches.

Laura Gross, you made the editorial process for this book so easy. Thank you for taking a product that was okay and making it so much better!

Thank you to Greg Stier from Dare 2 Share Ministries who has taken the concept of the "Pizza and God Talk" and shared it with thousands of youth workers across America. I appreciate your friendship and partnership.

Thank you to Leith Anderson and Ken Geis. I couldn't have asked for more gracious supervisors, mentors, and friends. You've encouraged me more than you'll ever know.

Finally, thank you to Cyndi, my precious wife. Once again you've given me the time I needed to complete this project. You've continued to believe in me and made me fall more in love with you each and every day. You are amazing.

Charlie was the head of the high school's philosophy club, a student of all religions, and a self-proclaimed agnostic. Jake and Becky were twin teenagers who were active in our student ministry. They had a huge burden for Charlie because they loved him and wanted him to know what it's like to experience Christ as they had. But Jake and Becky were afraid to invite Charlie to church. After all, he was an agnostic, so it wasn't like he'd come if they invited him.

But as much as they tried to dismiss their burden for Charlie, Jake and Becky just couldn't. The burden was too big. So they finally invited him, and much to their surprise, Charlie was thrilled to have an opportunity to go to a Christian church and hear what the pastor had to say. Jake and Becky couldn't believe it!

The twins were so excited the night Charlie came to our Wednesday night program. I'll never forget how they ran up to me before it began and pleaded with me to share the gospel that evening. They told me their friend Charlie was there, and they weren't sure if he'd ever walk into a church again.

11

They said, "You need to do this."

A gospel presentation didn't exactly fit in with the lesson that night (I was teaching on "How to Get Along with Your Parents"). However, I'd promised the students that if they ever brought a friend who needed Christ but they were afraid to share the gospel with that friend, then I'd work it into the lesson somehow.

I remember looking in Charlie's direction several times as I spoke. He was like a sponge soaking in every word I said. As I began to share about Christ's love for Charlie, his face grew somber and this tough agnostic softened. In a moment that can only be described as the Holy Spirit reaching out to one of God's children, Charlie accepted Christ as his Savior. No one could have predicted he would become a Christian. The circumstances behind Charlie's conversion were just too amazing.

I spoke with Charlie afterward and gave him a New Testament and some books for new Christians. The week that followed just flew by, and Charlie came back the next Wednesday night.

He said, "Hey Brian, you know that book you gave me? I read it! It was great!"

"Which one, Charlie? I gave you a few."

"The one that said *New Believers New Testament*."

"What do you mean you *read* it? Did you read a few pages?"

"No, I read the entire thing. From where it said, 'Now That You're a Christian,' through the book of Revelation. Do you have any more copies that I could give to my friends?"

I was floored. I'm a pastor, yet I've never read the entire New Testament in a week. But here was this high school guy who couldn't get enough. I probably gave Charlie 15 copies of the New Testament that first month, and he gave them all away. Within another month two of his friends had accepted Christ. Now Charlie was bringing atheists, agnostics, Wiccans, Shintos, Muslims, Mormons, Hindus, and more to our group. The questions these students had were deep. And it wasn't long before all of my preconceptions that students couldn't care less about theology were thrown away.

PIZZA AND GOD TALK

Charlie also e-mailed several questions to me each month. They dealt with everything from "Who are the Nephilim?" to "Could God create something so big that he couldn't lift it?" to "Why do Christians hate people who are gay?"

No matter what the topic, his questions would often require me to respond with four-to-five-page e-mails. I felt as though I was back in seminary again; only this time, I was writing papers for a 16-year-old kid. Interestingly enough, the 16-year-old asked better questions than my seminary professors did.

I felt Charlie's questions were important ones, and I wished every student in our ministry could read the e-mail dialogue Charlie and I were having. So I asked Charlie how he'd feel about getting together at a pizza place after our Wednesday night youth ministry for "Pizza and God Talk." We'd invite the rest of the group to come, and they could be part of our conversation. They could also ask whatever questions they had. And, since I knew I wouldn't know all the answers, I made this deal—the students had to answer the questions first. (But if any heresy started flying around, I'd be there to set things straight.)

The first week we had eight students. The next week we had nine. For week three we decided to do a special *Da Vinci Code* edition of "Pizza and God Talk." We had a whopping 11 students show up for that one, but the ball was rolling.

Today, 50 to 80 students meet every other week for "Pizza and God Talk." The simple concept has remained the same since week one—let students ask the questions that are on their minds. We've found that nothing else we do with high school students moves them along in their spiritual lives like this event. Why? Because "Pizza and God Talk" is discipleship that meets our students right where they're at today.

WHAT'S THE DEAL WITH *SEINFELD?*

This book is an amazing tool. It's best used with a Bible nearby, since it contains the questions our students have been asking since 2003—questions that explore both systematic and practical theology. Your students are probably asking the same things.

I love the comedy of Jerry Seinfeld. Many of Jerry's jokes begin with the phrase, "What's the deal with..." And I've found many of my students' questions about God begin this way too. Therefore, I've used that same format for all of the questions in this book.

When students answer the questions, I ask them to give me one of the following four reasons why they answered the way they did:

    1. Because of what the Bible says in _____.

    2. Because of personal experience.

    3. Because of what _____ told me.

    4. I don't know. I just believe it.

We tell our students from the beginning that some questions won't be answered until we get to heaven, while other answers will vary depending on a person's theological tradition.

Having said that, I should probably point out that this book has the potential to create divisiveness over petty issues (which is certainly not the intent). While most areas of theology are clear-cut, some are not. Therefore, we ask our students to respect each person's viewpoint. And the beautiful thing about students is they do a better job in this area than most adults I know.

Use this book, and it will transform your ministry. It might even change *you*. I'd love to hear how God uses this book in your ministry. E-mail your stories to brian_schulenburg@yahoo.com.

And if you'd like to submit questions for a future edition of this book, you may e-mail those to the same address. Each month I'll post the best questions on my blog at http://bschulenburg.blogspot.com.

May God bless you richly as you lead students closer to him.

Serving together with you,

Brian Schulenburg

1. What's the deal with Jesus? Why are there so many rumors about Jesus and Mary Magdalene?

2. What's the deal with the Bible? How do we know we can trust it?

3. What's the deal with the Nephilim? Who were they? Where did they come from? Could there still be Nephilim?

4. What's the deal with homosexuality? Why does the church get so uptight about it?

5. What's the deal with angels? Are they God's slaves?

6. What's the deal with free will? Do we really have one?

7. What's the deal with denominations? Why can't we all just get along?

8. What's the deal with church? Does God care whether or not I go? Does he care how often I go?

9. What's the deal with divorce? Did Jesus really say it was okay for non-Christians to divorce Christians because of their faith?

10. What's the deal with gambling? Is it okay or not?

11. What's the deal with heaven? Will there be sex in heaven?

12. What's the deal with dinosaurs? Were there dinosaurs on Noah's ark?

13. What's the deal with God's love? How could a loving God allow bad things to happen to good people?

14. What's the deal with church? Why does it seem so unimportant to so many people?

15. What's the deal with sin? Are some sins worse than others?

16. What's the deal with creation? How old is Earth?

17. What's the deal with hormones? If God doesn't want me to have sex before I'm married, why did he give me hormones?

18. What's the deal with God? Why do I feel so distant from him?

19. What's the deal with salvation? How does someone become a Christian?

20. What's the deal with hell? Why would God create people that he knew would go to hell?

21. What's the deal with swearing? Where in the Bible does it say anything about swearing? Who decides which words are curse words and which aren't?

22. What's the deal with alcohol? Why do some Christians say you shouldn't drink, while others say it's okay?

23. What's the deal with "chosen ones"? Does God really know who's going to become a Christian? Did he choose who the "chosen ones" would be? Why didn't he choose everyone?

24. What's the deal with forgiveness? Why are we supposed to ask God for forgiveness every day when he already forgave us once and for all?

25. What's the deal with God's love? Why would God let a baby die?

26. What's the deal with truth? Is there such a thing as absolute truth?

27. What's the deal with speaking in tongues? Are we supposed to do it?

28. What's the deal with Satan? Does he know where I am at all times?

29. What's the deal with demons? How does a person become possessed by a demon?

30. What's the deal with salvation? Can you lose your salvation?

31. What's the deal with hell? Is it really a lake of fire?

32. What's the deal with death? Where do you go when you die? Is purgatory real?

33. What's the deal with the Antichrist? Who will he be, and what will he do?

34. What's the deal with biblical prophecy? Are we supposed to take it literally or metaphorically?

35. What's the deal with sin? Will God continually forgive us for the same sins?

36. What's the deal with heaven? Can a sincere person of a non-Christian religion get there too?

37. What's the deal with church? Does it bug God that there are so many different denominations?

38. What's the deal with politics? Should churches be involved in politics?

39. What's the deal with the Trinity? How can God be three in one?

40. What's the deal with church? Is it important for students to go to "big church"?

41. What's the deal with heaven? Will married people still be married to each other when they're in heaven?

42. What's the deal with evangelism? How do I tell my friends about Jesus without totally offending them?

43. What's the deal with hell? What will it be like?

44. What's the deal with temptation? Can God be tempted?

45. What's the deal with Satan? Were Satan and Jesus friends at one time?

46. What's the deal with the Bible? Is it really without error?

47. What's the deal with music? Does God care what kind of music I listen to?

48. What's the deal with animals? Will my pet be in heaven?

49. What's the deal with dating? Is it a sin to date someone who isn't a Christian?

50. What's the deal with the planet Earth? Would Jesus drive an SUV?

51. What's the deal with God? Should I be afraid of him?

52. What's the deal with sex? Is it okay to have sex if you're engaged to the person?

53. What's the deal with the Bible? What does it mean when people say it's "inspired"?

54. What's the deal with God? Is he fair?

55. What's the deal with spiritual gifts? What are they, and how do I get one?

56. What's the deal with church? Why do some churches allow women to be pastors and others don't? Should women be allowed to teach men?

57. What's the deal with God's calling? How do you know if he's telling you to do something?

58. What's the deal with heaven? How can the Bible say there will be no more sorrow in heaven when some of my friends won't be there?

59. What's the deal with miracles? Why don't we see miracles today like we read about in the Bible?

60. What's the deal with religious people? Why does it seem as though Jesus didn't like them?

61. What's the deal with Adam and Eve's children? Whom did they marry?

62. What's the deal with the end times? What are the four horsemen of the Apocalypse?

63. What's the deal with Old Testament laws? Why don't we follow them today?

64. What's the deal with baptism? Why were people baptized before Jesus died and rose from the dead?

65. What's the deal with near-death experiences? People talk about seeing heaven or hell—is that possible?

66. What's the deal with God? Why would he allow someone like Paul to become a Christian but let my friend die and go to hell?

67. What's the deal with Jesus? Did he ever go on a date?

68. What's the deal with the Holy Spirit? What does it mean to be "filled with the Holy Spirit"?

69. What's the deal with heaven? Will everyone get rewards in heaven? Will some people get better rewards than others? Will that make people jealous?

70. What's the deal with speeding? Does God really care if we drive faster than the speed limit?

71. What's the deal with obedience? When is it okay to disobey my parents?

72. What's the deal with Ishmael? God said his descendents would be numerous. Who are they?

73. What's the deal with Jesus? If he's supposed to know everything, then why does the Bible say even Jesus doesn't know when he's coming back?

74. What's the deal with prayer? Can prayer change God's mind?

75. What's the deal with meditation? Is it some New Age thing, or are Christians supposed to meditate?

76. What's the deal with the disciple John? The Bible calls him the "beloved disciple." Does that mean Jesus loves some people more than he loves others?

77. What's the deal with Jesus? If he's God, then why did he have to pray?

78. What's the deal with evolution? Can you be a Christian and believe in evolution?

79. What's the deal with communion? Why do some churches teach that the bread and wine become the actual body of Christ inside of us, but other churches don't teach that? Which one's right?

80. What's the deal with abortion? Can you be a Christian and still believe a woman has a right to choose?

81. What's the deal with the end times? Who are the two witnesses?

82. What's the deal with the Holy Spirit? Is he a person?

83. What's the deal with doubt? Is it okay if I have doubts about my faith?

84. What's the deal with the planet Earth? Should Christians be concerned about global warming?

85. What's the deal with infant baptism? Why do some churches practice it and other churches don't? What does it symbolize?

86. What's the deal with babies who die? Do they go to heaven?

87. What's the deal with sin? When will I stop wanting to sin?

88. What's the deal with the end times? Why are there so many conflicting views about it? Why should I take the time to study it?

89. What's the deal with persecution? Does God really expect every Christian to go through persecution for their faith?

90. What's the deal with war? Is God okay with it?

91. What's the deal with people who claim God speaks to them? How do we know they're not just sharing their own agendas?

92. What's the deal with preachers? Why should we trust them when they're just human like everyone else?

93. What's the deal with spiritual gifts? Am I in danger of losing mine if I don't use it?

94. What's the deal with prayer? Can God hear my prayers if I have sin in my life?

95. What's the deal with the baptism of the Holy Spirit? What is it, and when does it take place?

96. What's the deal with homosexuality? Are people born homosexual?

97. What's the deal with worship? Does God really care what kind of music we use in our church?

98. What's the deal with joy? Why does it seem as though so many Christians don't have it?

99. What's the deal with the fruit of the Sprit? If I don't have all those characteristics in my life, does that mean I'm not a Christian?

100. What's the deal with me? Why did God make me this way?

101. What's the deal with decisions? How do I know I'm making the right one?

102. What's the deal with heaven? Will I play a harp in heaven?

103. What's the deal with marriage? Why did Paul say he wished people wouldn't get married?

104. What's the deal with divorce? Is it okay or not?

105. What's the deal with baptism? Are Christians supposed to be sprinkled or immersed?

106. What's the deal with testing? Does God test us?

107. What's the deal with people who never hear about Jesus? Will God send them to hell?

108. What's the deal with Mormons? Are they just another kind of Christian?

109. What's the deal with exercise? Does God want me to be physically fit?

110. What's the deal with movies? Is it okay for me to see whatever movie I want to see?

111. What's the deal with the kingdom of heaven? What is it?

112. What's the deal with church? Is one type of church better than another?

45

113. What's the deal with the resurrection? How do we know Jesus really rose from the dead?

114. What's the deal with faith? Is religion just a crutch for weak people?

115. What's the deal with the virgin birth? Why does it matter whether or not Mary had sex before Jesus was born?

116. What's the deal with hypocrites? Why should I follow Christ when there are so many hypocrites in my church?

117. What's the deal with Goliath? Why aren't there any giants around anymore?

118. What's the deal with Jesus? Why was he baptized?

119. What's the deal with God? How could a loving God tell the children of Israel to wipe out entire nations?

120. What's the deal with salvation? How did the people who lived before Jesus get to heaven?

121. What's the deal with polygamy? Was God okay with men having more than one wife in the Old Testament?

122. What's the deal with jobs? Is it okay for a Christian to work in an industry that might dishonor God?

123. What's the deal with the Sabbath? Am I supposed to take one?

124. What's the deal with idols? What would those look like today?

125. What's the deal with media? Would Jesus say we're too plugged in as a society, or would he like it?

126. What's the deal with lust? How is a person supposed to avoid it?

127. What's the deal with Wicca? Why is it growing so fast, and why is witchcraft appealing to teenagers?

128. What's the deal with the Great Commission? How are we supposed to accomplish it?

129. What's the deal with Judas? Is he in heaven or not?

130. What's the deal with religious people? Why are some people who've been very religious on earth going to hear Jesus say to them in heaven, "Get away from me, I never knew you"?

131. What's the deal with the Garden of Eden? Are the angels who guarded the entrance to the garden still there?

132. What's the deal with church? I don't like my church, what should I do?

133. What's the deal with discipleship? Has the church made it too easy to follow Jesus today?

134. What's the deal with patriotism? Is it a sin to be unpatriotic?

135. What's the deal with blessings? Why would God choose to bless Jacob and not Esau?

136. What's the deal with Mary and Martha? Why does it seem as though Jesus is scolding Martha when the work really had to get done?

137. What's the deal with spiritual gifts? What is the spiritual gift of prophecy and how is it used today?

138. What's the deal with the Bible? Why does the Catholic Bible have more books than the Protestant one? Which is right? Why?

139. What's the deal with church leaders? What disqualifies someone from serving in the church?

140. What's the deal with the Bible? Was the apostle Paul a male chauvinist?

141. What's the deal with fate? Is there such a thing?

142. What's the deal with prayer? Why do Catholics light candles when they pray?

143. What's the deal with the end times? Who is the false prophet?

144. What's the deal with the disciples? What happened to them?

145. What's the deal with all of those old people in the Bible? How did they live to be so old?

146. What's the deal with the end times? Some people are pretribulational, some are midtribulational, and others are post-tribulational—does it really matter?

147. What's the deal with Jesus? Did he descend to hell as the creeds say he did?

148. What's the deal with Muslims? Why do they seem to hate Christians so much?

149. What's the deal with Jewish people? Why were they God's chosen people? Are they still?

150. What's the deal with circumcision? Why would God make his people do that?

151. What's the deal with Job? Why did God make his life so miserable?

152. What's the deal with Solomon? If he was the wisest man to ever live, why did he do so many stupid things?

153. What's the deal with David? How could the Bible possibly say he was a man after God's own heart?

154. What's the deal with God? Why would he let the Pharaoh of Egypt and King Herod kill all those Hebrew babies?

155. What's the deal with Noah's ark? Why did God have to destroy the earth?

156. What's the deal with the transfiguration? What was that all about?

157. What's the deal with submission? Are women really supposed to submit to their husbands?

158. What's the deal with the Garden of Eden? What was it like? Did the animals in the garden talk to Adam?

159. What's the deal with omniscience? If God knows everything that's going to happen, why should I pray?

160. What's the deal with the ark of the covenant? Where is it today?

161. What's the deal with the Holy Grail? What is it?

162. What's the deal with Leonardo da Vinci? Was he part of a conspiracy to hide the truth about Jesus?

163. What's the deal with ambition? Is it a sin to be ambitious?

164. What's the deal with the Tower of Babel? Just how smart were the people who tried to build it?

165. What's the deal with heaven? Where is it?

166. What's the deal with hell? Where is it?

167. What's the deal with Abraham? Why did he keep asking his wife to tell people she was his sister?

168. What's the deal with Elijah and Enoch? Why didn't they die before they went to heaven?

169. What's the deal with parables? Why didn't Jesus make his teachings easier for everyone to understand?

170. What's the deal with Ananias and Sapphira? Why would God kill them for lying but not do the same to us?

171. What's the deal with the Bible? Is one version of the Bible better than the others?

172. What's the deal with angels? Do we all have guardian angels?

173. What's the deal with numbers? Why are certain numbers in the Bible special to God?

174. What's the deal with pigs? Why were they considered to be so bad?

175. What's the deal with sex? How far is too far?

176. What's the deal with visions? Does God speak to us in dreams or visions?

177. What's the deal with confession? Why do Catholics confess to a priest but Protestants don't confess to a pastor?

178. What's the deal with incense? Why do some churches use it, and what does it symbolize?

179. What's the deal with the Lord's Prayer? Are we supposed to pray it every day?

180. What's the deal with the age of accountability (a belief that God saves all those who die before they're "old enough" to make a decision for or against Christ)? Is there one?

181. What's the deal with sin? What's the unpardonable sin?

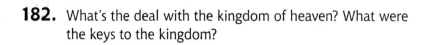

182. What's the deal with the kingdom of heaven? What were the keys to the kingdom?

183. What's the deal with the disciple Peter? Was he the first pope?

184. What's the deal with salvation? What role do I play in my salvation?

185. What's the deal with God? Who is God?

186. What's the deal with sin? Did God create sin?

187. What's the deal with Satan? Why did God create him?

188. What's the deal with temptation? If God doesn't tempt us, why did he put the Tree of Knowledge of Good and Evil in the Garden of Eden?

189. What's the deal with the rich young ruler? Why did Jesus tell him to sell everything he had if he wanted to have eternal life?

190. What's the deal with the church offering? Why does God need our money?

191. What's the deal with God? Why did he make some people really attractive and others not so much?

192. What's the deal with witches? Where do they get their power? Should Christians fear them?

193. What's the deal with the Bible? If there are a bunch of inconsistencies in the Bible, does that prove the Bible is full of errors?

194. What's the deal with disabilities? Why would God allow some people to suffer so much?

195. What's the deal with the guy in hell who asked to have a drink of water? Can someone see heaven from hell and vice versa?

196. What's the deal with Mary? Why do Catholics pray to her and Protestants don't?

197. What's the deal with worship? How would God define it?

198. What's the deal with money? Is the love of it really the root of all evil?

199. What's the deal with demons? Why would some angels choose to reject God?

200. What's the deal with heaven? Can you choose to reject God or choose to sin once you get to heaven (like Satan and the demons did)?

201. What's the deal with the ark of the covenant? What was kept inside it? Why were people struck dead for touching it?

202. What's the deal with God? Does he have an ego?

203. What's the deal with salvation? What did Paul mean when he said to "work out your salvation with fear and trembling" (Philippians 2:12)?

204. What's the deal with Balaam's donkey? Why could this animal see the angel? Why was the animal able to talk?

205. What's the deal with prayer? Why does it seem as though sometimes it's answered and sometimes it's not?

206. What's the deal with spiritual warfare? Are angels and demons involved in some sort of behind-the-scenes cosmic battle? Do our prayers impact the outcome?

207. What's the deal with Scientology? Why does it seem like so many Hollywood stars become Scientologists?

208. What's the deal with Satan? Can the Devil make us do something?

209. What's the deal with God? Does he love Christians more than he loves non-Christians?

210. What's the deal with Santa Claus and the Easter Bunny? Is it okay for Christians to celebrate Christmas and Easter using these symbols?

211. What's the deal with space? How do the heavens declare the glory of God?

212. What's the deal with immorality? Who determines what's immoral and what isn't?

213. What's the deal with Christian television? Why is it of such poor quality?

214. What's the deal with cliques? Why does it seem as though my youth group has so many of them?

215. What's the deal with forgiveness? How do I forgive someone when I don't feel like doing it?

216. What's the deal with Satan? What does he look like?

217. What's the deal with God? Why does he allow hunger and famine?

218. What's the deal with the pope? Could he possibly be infallible?

71

219. What's the deal with MySpace? Would Jesus have a MySpace account?

220. What's the deal with angels and demons? Do we have an angel sitting on one shoulder and a demon on the other?

221. What's the deal with God? Can he make something so big that he can't lift it?

222. What's the deal with the disciples? Is it possible they were all just delusional?

223. What's the deal with Jesus? If he drank wine, then why can't I?

224. What's the deal with Lot's wife? Why would God turn her into a pillar of salt? Why was her punishment so harsh?

225. What's the deal with Satan? Does he still have free access to God?

226. What's the deal with gods? How do you know if you've made something into a god in your life?

227. What's the deal with terrorism? Does God love terrorists?

228. What's the deal with racism? Why does it seem as though racism never gets any better?

229. What's the deal with love? How do I love my enemies?

230. What's the deal with secret societies? Are they evil?

231. What's the deal with Satan? Is Satan sin incarnate, or is sin something else altogether?

232. What's the deal with Solomon's Temple? Why did God want such an elaborate building?

233. What's the deal with church? Is it okay for churches to spend millions of dollars on a building?

234. What's the deal with conflict? How am I supposed to deal with conflict with another Christian?

235. What's the deal with the Holy Spirit? Is he my conscience?

236. What's the deal with marriage? Is it okay for a Christian pastor to preside over the wedding of a Christian who marries a non-Christian?

237. What's the deal with school? Should Christians take their children out of public schools?

238. What's the deal with political activism? How involved with politics should Christians and churches be?

239. What's the deal with church pews? Do they say something about our theology of worship?

240. What's the deal with prayer? Are we supposed to kneel before God?

241. What's the deal with church? Why do so many people dress up for it? Does God care about what we wear to church?

242. What's the deal with tithes and offerings? Is there a difference between them?

243. What's the deal with mission trips? Are short-term mission trips a waste of money? Would it be more helpful to send the money we raise directly to the people who really need it, rather than buying airplane tickets, food, and supplies for the mission team members?

244. What's the deal with respect? Why does it seem as though none of my Christian friends respect God?

245. What's the deal with Jesus? Why did he have to die?

246. What's the deal with popularity? Is it okay for a Christian to want to be popular?

247. What's the deal with violent video games? Is it okay for Christians to play games where people are shot and killed?

248. What's the deal with forgiveness? Would God expect someone who'd been the victim of a violent crime to forgive the offender?

249. What's the deal with contemplative prayer? Is it a bad thing?

250. What's the deal with Catholic saints? How does one become a saint?

251. What's the deal with abortion? Would God be okay with a woman having an abortion in the case of rape or incest?

252. What's the deal with smoking? Why do so many Christians make a big deal about it? How do the effects of smoking compare with the effects of overeating or drinking too much coffee?

253. What's the deal with parental discipline? Is it okay for parents to spank their children?

254. What's the deal with the Ten Commandments? Can anyone keep all of them?

255. What's the deal with church? Is it okay to be excited to see my friends at church, or is it supposed to be all about God?

256. What's the deal with suicide? If someone takes his own life, does he go to hell?

257. What's the deal with God? If he is all-powerful, why doesn't he defeat evil once and for all?

258. What's the deal with the Dead Sea Scrolls? Why are they such a significant find?

259. What's the deal with Jesus? I've heard some people say he may have never existed. Is it possible he's just an elaborate hoax?

260. What's the deal with the Messiah? Why don't most Jewish people believe Jesus is the Messiah?

261. What's the deal with other religions? If a lot of other religions also have Christlike figures and stories about their "saviors" rising from the dead, then how do we know we're right and they're wrong?

262. What's the deal with Mormons? Why do they seem so much more committed to their faith than Christians do?

263. What's the deal with salvation? How does each member of the Trinity play a role in our salvation?

264. What's the deal with the Apostles' Creed? How did it come about?

265. What's the deal with Western Christianity? Is it true the rest of the Christian world doesn't like how Christianity is practiced in the West? Why?

266. What's the deal with mental health? Is it okay for Christians to seek help from psychologists, psychiatrists, or counselors?

267. What's the deal with yoga? Is yoga an okay thing for Christians to do?

268. What's the deal with agnostics? What do they believe?

269. What's the deal with the Bible? Did God just tell the writers of Scripture what to put on the scroll and they wrote it?

270. What's the deal with Jehovah's Witnesses? What do they believe?

271. What's the deal with postmodernism? How will it affect the church for years to come?

272. What's the deal with God? Why is he silent about so many issues that people care deeply about?

273. What's the deal with man? If we're created in the image of God, does that mean we'll be just like him someday?

274. What's the deal with history? Is there historical proof of the things we read about in the Bible from sources *other* than the Bible?

275. What's the deal with the exodus? Are chariots sitting on the bottom of the Red Sea?

276. What's the deal with Iraq? Is it talked about in the Bible?

277. What's the deal with mankind? Are we born sinners?

278. What's the deal with the temple? Is it ever going to be rebuilt? Will it be on top of the Dome of the Rock?

279. What's the deal with Israel? Will it ever become the nation it once was under King David?

280. What's the deal with the end times? Referring to the millennial reign of Christ, what does it mean to be premillennial, amillennial, or postmillennial?

281. What's the deal with dispensationalism? I've heard the word before, but I have no idea what it means.

282. What's the deal with religion? Are we in trouble if we're not actively taking care of widows and orphans?

283. What's the deal with money? Is it okay to be rich and a Christian?

284. What's the deal with gossip? Why don't more churches discipline people for gossiping?

285. What's the deal with the seven deadly sins? Does God think they're worse than any other sins?

286. What's the deal with Babylon? Where was it, and will it rise again?

287. What's the deal with demons? Is it possible to see one?

288. What's the deal with angels? I think I may have had an encounter with one—is that possible?

289. What's the deal with visions of Jesus? I've heard all these stories about Jesus appearing to Muslims in their dreams and telling them he's God. Is that possible?

290. What's the deal with the gospel? Is it true that Jesus will return after the gospel has been preached to every people group on earth?

291. What's the deal with food? Why do Catholics eat fish on Fridays? What is kosher food?

292. What's the deal with mega-churches? Do they hurt the overall church by creating "consumer Christians" and stealing people away from smaller churches?

293. What's the deal with fasting? Why would anyone want to do that?

294. What's the deal with Muslims? Why do they take a pilgrimage? Should Christians take pilgrimages too?

295. What's the deal with solitude? Is it an important thing to have in the Christian life?

296. What's the deal with living together before marriage? Is it okay for a couple to live together if they're not having sex?

297. What's the deal with homosexuality? Why are so many denominations ordaining homosexual clergy?

298. What's the deal with pastors and priests? Why can pastors marry but priests cannot?

299. What's the deal with Catholics and Protestants? Why do so many of them think the other ones are going to hell?

300. What's the deal with marriage? Should it really be defined as only the union between a man and a woman?

301. What's the deal with homosexuality? Why do so many Christians think homosexuals shouldn't be allowed to claim their partners as dependents for health care benefits?

302. What's the deal with pastors? Why do some denominations make pastors change churches every few years?

303. What's the deal with the religious right? Why do they seem so mean?

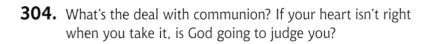

304. What's the deal with communion? If your heart isn't right when you take it, is God going to judge you?

305. What's the deal with the Old Testament? Do the promises from the Old Testament apply to us?

306. What's the deal with hunting? Is it okay to hunt animals when God told us to take care of the earth?

307. What's the deal with education? Is it better for Christians to go to a Christian college or a secular university?

308. What's the deal with the death penalty? Should Christians be in favor of it?

309. What's the deal with priorities? If I have school activities that conflict with church activities, which ones should take precedence?

310. What's the deal with God? How does he hear everyone's prayers at the same time?

311. What's the deal with poverty? How should Christians respond to it?

312. What's the deal with joy and happiness? Are they the same thing?

313. What's the deal with Jesus? Why did Jesus weep when he heard that Lazarus had died—especially since Jesus knew he'd raise Lazarus from the dead?

314. What's the deal with last rites? Why do Catholic priests offer them to people, and what happens if they're not read?

315. What's the deal with marriage? Why is it so important to God?

316. What's the deal with God? Why does he allow violence to go on all over the world?

317. What's the deal with faith? Does God make it easy for us to believe?

318. What's the deal with the Bible? Is it possible that new books could be added today, such as the Book of Mormon?

319. What's the deal with angels? What do they do all day?

320. What's the deal with spiritual gifts? Are some more important than others?

321. What's the deal with euthanasia? Is there ever a time when it should be considered merciful to take someone's life?

322. What's the deal with homosexuality? Should Christians support homosexuals who are in loving, monogamous relationships? Is that better than heterosexual Christians who sleep around?

323. What's the deal with elders? Are they supposed to be in charge of the church?

WHAT'S THE DEAL WITH...

324. What's the deal with sex? Is oral sex okay?

325. What's the deal with bar mitzvahs and bat mitzvahs? Why are they such a big deal to Jewish people?

326. What's the deal with evangelism? How do you share Christ with an atheist?

327. What's the deal with pastors? Should a pastor who's been caught having an affair be allowed to preach again?

328. What's the deal with *Lectio Divina*? What is it, and should Christians do it?

329. What's the deal with celibacy? Why aren't priests and nuns allowed to marry anyone?

330. What's the deal with the Middle East? Why do all those countries hate Israel so much?

331. What's the deal with church planting? Do we need more churches in the world?

332. What's the deal with the plagues? Why did God choose to work in such harsh ways?

333. What's the deal with Song of Solomon? Why is there such an erotic book in the Bible?

334. What's the deal with fame? Is it a bad thing to pursue fame?

335. What's the deal with nudity? Is it okay for Christians to view nudity in movies or art?

336. What's the deal with the film *The Passion of the Christ*? Why did it make so many people so angry?

337. What's the deal with Ouija boards? Will you really become demon-possessed if you use one?

338. What's the deal with Satanism? What do Satanists believe?

339. What's the deal with fashion? Does God care about what I wear?

340. What's the deal with revenge? When is it okay to seek revenge?

341. What's the deal with anger? How do you not sin when you're angry?

342. What's the deal with Jesus? Would he have really died if I were the only person to ever live?

343. What's the deal with sacrifice? Why did God require sacrifices in Old Testament times?

344. What's the deal with Christianity? Is it easier to live life as a Christian or as a non-Christian?

345. What's the deal with love? How do you find someone who'll love you with the kind of love the Bible talks about?

346. What's the deal with courtship? Should I really kiss dating goodbye?

347. What's the deal with media piracy? Is it really a big deal if I copy media files from my friends?

348. What's the deal with prisoners? I thought I read something in the Bible about Christians helping them— am I supposed to be helping them?

349. What's the deal with hell? When was it created?

350. What's the deal with faith? Is faith without choice really faith?

351. What's the deal with Satan? Where is he today?

352. What's the deal with Unitarians? What do they believe?

353. What's the deal with genuflecting? Why don't Protestants genuflect?

354. What's the deal with prophecy? Are there prophets today?

355. What's the deal with Reformed theology? What is it?

356. What's the deal with forgiveness? Are you supposed to forgive people who've abused you—even if they haven't asked for your forgiveness?

357. What's the deal with hypocrisy? Is it possible to be a Christian and *not* be a hypocrite?

358. What's the deal with angels and demons? Why don't we see them like people did back in Bible times?

359. What's the deal with temptation? Does God really provide a way of escape every time I'm tempted?

360. What's the deal with church? Am I a sinner if I think it's boring?

361. What's the deal with gluttony? Does God care about how much people weigh?

362. What's the deal with God the Father? Is there a Mother God?

363. What's the deal with Satan? I heard he was in charge of the music when he was in heaven. Is that true?

364. What's the deal with sex? Is masturbation okay?

365. What's the deal with Jesus? Did he appear in the Old Testament?

366. What's the deal with archeology? How do archeological finds support what we read in the Bible?

367. What's the deal with Ruth? If God doesn't want me sleeping with someone of the opposite sex, then why did Naomi tell Ruth to spend the night with Boaz?

368. What's the deal with animals? What kind of rights should they have?

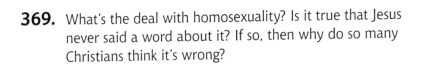

369. What's the deal with homosexuality? Is it true that Jesus never said a word about it? If so, then why do so many Christians think it's wrong?

370. What's the deal with vegetarianism? Would Jesus have been a vegetarian?

371. What's the deal with angels and demons? When were they created?

372. What's the deal with salvation? Is there really only one way to God, or are there multiple ways to find salvation?

373. What's the deal with the Gospel of Judas? Should it be considered a book of the Bible?

374. What's the deal with the Gnostic Gospels? I've heard there should be a lot more books included in the Bible. Is that true?

375. What's the deal with Allah? Is he the same God whom Christians worship?

376. What's the deal with cults? What makes a religion a cult?

377. What's the deal with God? Why did he send Jesus to earth when he did? Would it have made more sense to send Jesus after cameras had been invented? Then people could have recorded evidence of his miracles.

378. What's the deal with missionaries? Why do the ones I meet seem so strange?

379. What's the deal with evangelism? If I don't have the spiritual gift of evangelism, does God really expect me to witness to others?

380. What's the deal with mankind? Are we all basically good or evil?

381. What's the deal with music? Why does it seem as though Satan has all the good music?

382. What's the deal with church? What does it mean when churches say they're liberal or conservative?

383. What's the deal with culture? Is the gospel a friend or foe of our culture?

384. What's the deal with God? Why would he allow a child to be abused?

385. What's the deal with Adam? How did he find all of the animals he named?

386. What's the deal with hell? Does hell end?

387. What's the deal with eternity? What will it look like for Christians and non-Christians?

388. What's the deal with the Holy Spirit? If we're created in the image of God, and if the Holy Spirit *is* God, then does the Holy Spirit have a body?

389. What's the deal with the plagues? Why was God so cruel to the Egyptian people?

390. What's the deal with school? Does God care about my grades?

391. What's the deal with judgment? How does God's judgment work? Will Satan and his demons be punished worse than non-Christians will be?

392. What's the deal with sin? Will God play a recording of my sins on a giant TV screen in heaven for all to see?

393. What's the deal with baptism? Is it a sin not to be baptized?

394. What's the deal with medical research? Is stem cell research an okay thing for Christians to support?

395. What's the deal with books and movies like *The Da Vinci Code*? Is it okay for Christians to read or watch them?

396. What's the deal with the number 666? Why do some people think it's Satan's number?

397. What's the deal with grace? Can a true Christian ever fall away from the grace of God?

398. What's the deal with Jesus? Is it bad if I'm not excited about his return and I really want him to wait until after I've been married to come back to earth?

399. What's the deal with confession? If a murderer confesses to a priest that he killed someone, does the priest have a moral responsibility to tell the authorities?

400. What's the deal with God? Why would he tell Hosea to marry a prostitute?

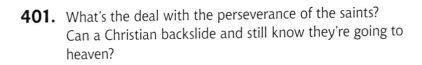

401. What's the deal with the perseverance of the saints? Can a Christian backslide and still know they're going to heaven?

402. What's the deal with Jesus? Is it possible that he appeared to more people than just the ones living in what's now known as Israel?

403. What's the deal with the Tree of Life? What would have happened to Adam and Eve if they'd eaten from it?

404. What's the deal with reincarnation? Will we be reincarnated?

405. What's the deal with Lazarus? Where did his soul go between the time he died and when Jesus raised him from the dead four days later?

406. What's the deal with heaven? Why do we need a new heaven after the thousand-year reign of Christ?

407. What's the deal with slavery? Why does it seem as though the Bible endorses it?

408. What's the deal with God? Why does the Bible say he hardened Pharaoh's heart?

409. What's the deal with human cloning? If humans are ever cloned, will the clones have souls?

410. What's the deal with the spiritual gift of discernment? How do you know if you have it?

411. What's the deal with the phrase, "Oh my God!"? Does saying it really break one of the Ten Commandments?

412. What's the deal with heaven? What language will we speak in heaven?

413. What's the deal with Jehovah's Witnesses? Are they just like another Christian denomination?

414. What's the deal with prayer? I know some people say they have prayer languages. What is that?

415. What's the deal with death? Do angels show us the way to heaven when we die?

416. What's the deal with patience? Why does God make us wait for so many good things?

417. What's the deal with self-control? How does that connect to living a Spirit-controlled life?

418. What's the deal with Christians? Why do so many of them fall into sin?

419. What's the deal with Satan? What does it mean that he's the "prince of this world"?

420. What's the deal with God? Can God change his mind?

421. What's the deal with fraternities and sororities? Should Christians get involved with them?

422. What's the deal with Jesus? Why did he pray for himself in the third person in John 17?

423. What's the deal with natural disasters? Why would God plan for them to happen as he says in Micah 2?

424. What's the deal with omnipresence? How can God be everywhere at once?

425. What's the deal with God? If he really sees everything I do, then how could he possibly love me?

426. What's the deal with the Masons and Masonic Lodges? Are they some sort of cult?

427. What's the deal with cults? If cults are organizations that teach incorrect doctrine and if every church denomination has doctrinal differences, does that mean we're all part of some kind of cult?

428. What's the deal with people like Billy Graham? Why does God seem to do such extraordinary things through some people yet not through others?

429. What's the deal with being a martyr? Is it true that there's a special reward in heaven for those who are martyred for their faith?

430. What's the deal with God? Can God hate?

431. What's the deal with our body, soul, and spirit? What's the difference between the soul and the spirit?

432. What's the deal with animals? Do they have souls?

433. What's the deal with the woman caught in adultery? Does the fact that Jesus didn't judge her mean he doesn't really care about our sins?

434. What's the deal with a one-world religion? Is that ever going to happen?

435. What's the deal with intolerance? What should Christians be intolerant about, and what should they tolerate?

436. What's the deal with salvation? My sister just married a Mormon and converted to Mormonism. Does that mean she lost her salvation?

437. What's the deal with God? Why did he wrestle with Jacob? What was that all about?

438. What's the deal with angels? Are they male or female?

439. What's the deal with altar calls ("coming forward" to make a decision for Christ) during a church service? Why do some churches do that every week and others never do it?

440. What's the deal with prayer? Does God get mad when we pray for a particular team to win a ball game?

441. What's the deal with healing? Why should I ask God to heal my sick friend when he chooses *not* to heal people more often than he chooses to heal them?

442. What's the deal with the millennial reign of Christ? Will people become Christians during that time?

443. What's the deal with praying over and laying hands on missionaries? Why do churches do that?

444. What's the deal with prayer? Why do the elders and pastors in some churches pray over the sick and anoint them with oil?

445. What's the deal with obedience? If my parents tell me to eat everything on my plate but I don't do it, am I living in sin?

446. What's the deal with ghosts? Are they real, and should Christians fear them?

447. What's the deal with Jesus? Somebody said there's a verse in the Bible that says Jesus wasn't attractive. Was Jesus ugly?

448. What's the deal with happiness? Does God want us to be happy?

449. What's the deal with preaching? If we have the Bible, why do we need someone preaching to us? Shouldn't the Bible be all we need?

450. What's the deal with Jesus? Was he "just a prophet," as Islam teaches?

451. What's the deal with God? Why did he leave us so many mysteries about himself?

452. What's the deal with salvation? Can someone who's never heard the name of Jesus be saved?

453. What's the deal with fanaticism? Is there a point where Christians cross the line in their dedication to God?

454. What's the deal with the law? Who determines which laws are still relevant for today and which aren't?

455. What's the deal with government? How can a country be called a "Christian nation"?

456. What's the deal with sin? What are the consequences of my sins?

457. What's the deal with angels? Can they have sex? If not, then why do some people think the Nephilim were fallen angels?

458. What's the deal with mankind? Are men and women created equal?

459. What's the deal with wisdom? Does God really promise to give it to us if we ask for it? How do we know whether or not we've received it?

460. What's the deal with God? Why did he make all of the things that look so fun the very things we aren't supposed to do?

461. What's the deal with authority in the church? What do I do when I disagree with the direction in which the church leaders are taking us?

462. What's the deal with parental discipline? How should parents discipline their children?

463. What's the deal with missionaries? How do they decide where God is calling them to serve?

464. What's the deal with fasting? Is it okay for someone who's struggled with eating disorders to fast?

465. What's the deal with cutting? Is it possible that people who cut themselves are being influenced by demons?

466. What's the deal with faith healers? Is that stuff on TV real, or is it a hoax?

467. What's the deal with the millennial reign of Christ? Will people who are alive during that time die, or will they live for a thousand years?

468. What's the deal with Ananias and Sapphira? Are they in heaven?

469. What's the deal with Jesus? Why didn't people (like Mary and the two disciples) recognize him right away when they saw his resurrected body?

470. What's the deal with the Crusades? Will God judge more harshly those who were involved in the Crusades for the things people did in his name?

471. What's the deal with catechisms? Should we put as much trust in them as we put in the Bible?

472. What's the deal with the stations of the cross? Did all of those events really happen as Jesus carried his cross?

473. What's the deal with God? Why does it seem as though he can be so unfair in his treatment of us?

474. What's the deal with biblical prophecy? Is the United States mentioned in the prophetic portions of the Bible?

475. What's the deal with the Antichrist? Could he be alive today?

476. What's the deal with the harlot who's mentioned in the book of Revelation? What's her role in Bible prophecy?

477. What's the deal with the Holy Spirit? What does it mean to "grieve the Holy Spirit"?

478. What's the deal with exorcism? Is it biblical?

479. What's the deal with the Christian life? How can anyone possibly live the kind of life that the Bible seems to indicate we should live?

480. What's the deal with ghosts? Is it possible for a house to be haunted?

481. What's the deal with the four Gospels? If there are discrepancies between them, does that prove the writers of the Gospels each had their own agendas?

482. What's the deal with eternity? After a few thousand years, will we all just want to be done with life?

483. What's the deal with religion? Is it the most divisive force on earth?

484. What's the deal with salvation? How can you have a relationship with a God you cannot see or hear?

485. What's the deal with angels? Do they have wings?

486. What's the deal with government? What's separation of church and state all about?

487. What's the deal with modesty? Is it okay for girls to wear bikinis?

488. What's the deal with Jesus? Why did he cast the demons out of that one guy and into a herd of pigs?

489. What's the deal with wealth? Why did Jesus say it was so hard for those who are rich to enter the kingdom of heaven?

490. What's the deal with lust? Is it true that if I look at a woman with lust in my heart, I've committed adultery with her?

491. What's the deal with Adam? What would have happened if he *didn't* eat from the Tree of the Knowledge of Good and Evil, but Eve did?

492. What's the deal with abortion? Should Christians protest in front of abortion clinics?

493. What's the deal with unity? Why does it seem as though Christians are always fighting?

494. What's the deal with Bible study? What's the best way to study the Bible?

495. What's the deal with spiritual disciplines? What are they?

496. What's the deal with Jesus? When did he know he was the Son of God and the Son of Man?

497. What's the deal with Christian community? Is it okay if my best friends aren't Christians?

498. What's the deal with prayer? Is there a certain formula for prayer?

499. What's the deal with planning for the future? Someone I know says God gets upset if we make plans for our future. Is that true?

500. What's the deal with this book? If you have a question for the next *What's the Deal With...* book, send it to brian_schulenburg@yahoo.com. Each month Brian will post the best questions on his blog, *Pass the Salt,* which you can find at http://bschulenburg.blogspot.com.

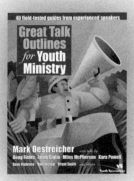
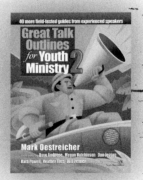